WOMEN WHO DARE

Marian Anderson

BY HOWARD S. KAPLAN

Pomegranate

SAN FRANCISCO

LIBRARY OF CONGRESS
WASHINGTON, DC

Published by Pomegranate Communications, Inc.
Box 808022, Petaluma CA 94975
800 227 1428; www.pomegranate.com

Pomegranate Europe Ltd.
Unit 1, Heathcote Business Centre, Hurlbutt Road
Warwick, Warwickshire CV34 6TD, UK
[+44] 0 1926 430111; sales@pomeurope.co.uk

Amy Pastan, Series Editor

In association with the Library of Congress, Pomegranate publishes other books in the Women Who Dare® series, as well as calendars, books of postcards, posters, and Knowledge Cards® featuring daring women. Please contact the publisher for more information.

Library of Congress Cataloging-in-Publication Data

Kaplan, Howard S. (Howard Stephen), 1960–
   Marian Anderson / by Howard S. Kaplan.
      p. cm. — (Women who dare)
   Includes bibliographical references (p.   ).
   ISBN-13: 978-0-7649-3891-7
   1. Anderson, Marian, 1897–1993. 2. Contraltos—United States—Biography. I. Title.

   ML420.A6K37 2007
   782.109—dc22
   [B]
                                                      2006048651

Pomegranate Catalog No. A133
Designed by Harrah Lord, Yellow House Studio, Rockport, ME
Printed in Korea

16 15 14 13 12 11 10 09 08 07   10 9 8 7 6 5 4 3 2 1

FRONT COVER: *Marian Anderson in Vienna, 1934.* LC-USZ62-66161
BACK COVER: *Legendary conductor of the Philadelphia Orchestra Leopold Stokowski conducts the Westminster Choir College Choir as Marian Anderson sings "Ave Maria" for a filmed Christmas concert, 1944.*
ANNENBERG RARE BOOK AND MANUSCRIPT LIBRARY, UNIVERSITY OF PENNSYLVANIA

PREFACE

FOR TWO HUNDRED YEARS, the Library of Congress, the oldest national cultural institution in the United States, has been gathering materials necessary to tell the stories of women in America. The last third of the twentieth century witnessed a great surge of popular and scholarly interest in women's studies and women's history that has led to an outpouring of works in many formats. Drawing on women's history resources in the collections of the Library of Congress, the Women Who Dare book series is designed to provide readers with an entertaining introduction to the life of a notable American woman or a significant topic in women's history.

From its beginnings in 1800 as a legislative library, the Library of Congress has grown into a national library that houses both a universal collection of knowledge and the mint record of American creativity. Congress' decision to purchase Thomas Jefferson's personal library to replace the books and maps burned during the British occupation in 1814 set the Congressional Library on the path of collecting with the breadth of Jefferson's interests. Not just American imprints were to be acquired, but foreign-language materials as well, and Jefferson's library already included works by American and European women.

The Library of Congress has some 121 million items, largely housed in closed stacks in three buildings on Capitol Hill that contain twenty public reading rooms. The incredible, wide-ranging collections include books, maps, prints, newspapers, broadsides, diaries, letters, posters, musical scores, photographs, audio and video recordings, and documents available only in digital formats. The Library serves first-time users and the most experienced researchers alike.

I hope that you, the reader, will seek and find in the pages of this book information that will further your understanding of women's history. In addition, I hope you will continue to explore the topic of this book in a library near you, in person at the Library of Congress, or by visiting the Library on the World Wide Web at http://www.loc.gov. Happy reading!

—JAMES H. BILLINGTON, The Librarian of Congress

On a cold and windy Sunday afternoon in April 1939, Marian Anderson stood at a specially built podium with a tall stand of microphones in front of her. She walked out to the steps of the Lincoln Memorial; the massive figure of the former president was, perhaps, the most imposing member of the vast audience awaiting her performance. She looked elegant in her mink coat and flowing orange-and-yellow scarf. With a sultry contralto voice as dark as midnight but as uplifting as a new day, Anderson began to sing. The extraordinary tones touched the hearts of the more than seventy-five thousand people gathered before her, as well as the multitudes listening on their home radios. At that moment, she seemed older than her forty-two years; she seemed timeless—a messenger of peace, hope, and promise. With the first notes of "America" and the songs that followed, Anderson went from singer to symbol, representing the quest for freedom and civil rights so long denied to Americans of African descent.

■ *Anderson stands before the statue of President Abraham Lincoln as her concert on the National Mall brings the issue of civil rights and equality to the forefront of American society.* GETTY IMAGES

■ *Marian Anderson, the "baby contralto," in 1898, one year old. "I think music chose me," she would later say.*

THE BABY CONTRALTO

JUST DECADES after the Civil War ended, Marian Anderson came into the world on February 27, 1897, in Philadelphia. She was the first of three girls born to John and Anna Anderson, who had moved north from Virginia as part of the Great Migration, in which black families fled the South in search of a better life. Life in Philadelphia was better, but not always easier. Only a year before Anderson's birth, the Supreme Court had ruled famously in favor of "separate but equal" institutions for blacks and whites, making racial segregation the law of the land.

John Anderson supported his family by selling coal and ice at the Reading Terminal Market. Anderson remembered her father as handsome, tall, and dark, of just the right build. Her mother, on the other hand, was "tiny" and had to stand on tiptoe to help her father put on his tie. Just before their second child, Alyse, was born, the Andersons moved into John's mother's house. When baby Ethel arrived, the family moved to a larger space on nearby Colorado Street.

Every Sunday, Marian Anderson went to the Union Baptist Church, which would prove to nourish not only her soul but her budding career as well. After she turned six, she became a member of the church's junior choir, which was under the direction of Alexander Robinson, one of the first people to recognize Anderson's unusual voice. Before long, everybody in the congregation knew that she had something special: she could sing the high soprano parts, but she also had the velvety, dark timbre of a contralto, the lowest female singing voice.

■ *Marian Anderson (seated, center); her mother, Anna (standing); and her sisters, Alyse (left) and Ethel (right), c. 1910. The close-knit family was determined to offer the talented Marian a chance to realize her dream as a singer.* ANNENBERG RARE BOOK AND MANUSCRIPT LIBRARY, UNIVERSITY OF PENNSYLVANIA

A HOME FULL OF MUSIC

Music always seemed to fill the Anderson house. While he dressed in the morning, Anderson's father used to sing an old parlor song from the 1890s, "Asleep in the Deep." Her mother used to sing as well, and when the weather prevented the family from going outside, she and the girls would sing "old American songs, hymns, and spirituals" to entertain themselves.

At public school it was all Anderson could do to keep from singing. The music room was next to her classroom, and she listened carefully to the sounds coming through

■ *John Berkley Anderson, Marian's father, in the 1890s.* ANNENBERG RARE BOOK AND MANUSCRIPT LIBRARY, UNIVERSITY OF PENNSYLVANIA

the wall, eagerly anticipating the time when she and her classmates could visit the music room. When she was eight, her father bought a piano from his brother. The family had no money for piano lessons, however, so Anderson learned as best she could. She used to sit on her father's lap while she tried out the scales. She also became interested in the violin and bought her first one in a pawn shop for $3.98.

As a young girl, Anderson began scrubbing the steps of houses in her South Philadelphia neighborhood to earn money. If she scrubbed a whole set of steps, she could make as much as a nickel. She also delivered the laundry that her mother took in. Once, the young Anderson was delivering a basket of freshly cleaned clothes when she heard the notes of a familiar instrument coming from an open window. She set down the basket, looked in the window, and saw a woman at the piano with skin as dark as hers. That experience gave Anderson resolve: "I realized that if *she* could, *I* could." She never gave up such resolve throughout her long career, and, in fact, inspired it in others.

Anderson's aunt Mary, in an effort to help a struggling church, agreed to put together a concert to help raise money for the building fund. Anderson did not find out about her own participation in the concert until she happened across a flyer on the sidewalk. "Come and hear the baby contralto, ten years old," it read, with Anderson's name and picture included. The eight-year-old was thrilled not only to be given star billing at a concert but also to be presented as a slightly older child. She was so excited that she returned home from the grocer with potatoes instead of the bread that her mother had requested. Anna Anderson gently turned her daughter around and sent her back out to the store.

The "baby contralto" was also asked to join the People's Chorus, made up of singers from black churches all over Philadelphia. Though just one of one hundred voices, Anderson's contralto clearly set her apart from most of the other singers. In case she was too small to be seen, the chorus director, Emma Azalia Hackley, insisted that Anderson stand on a chair for her solo. "I want her to feel elevated," Hackley said, "and I want no one in the back of the hall to have the slightest difficulty in seeing her."

A HOUSE FULL OF WOMEN

In 1909, tragedy struck the Anderson household. John Anderson was accidentally hit in the head at work, a blow that proved to be fatal. He died at home shortly after Christmas. The twelve-year-old Anderson and her family had no choice but to move in with her paternal grandparents, who lived on nearby Fitzwater Street. Her grandmother, Isabella Anderson, was a strong-willed woman, "the boss," while her grandfather, Benjamin Anderson, appeared more quiet. And while the rest of the family were Baptists, he referred to himself as a "black Jew" and observed the Sabbath on Saturday, as well as holidays such as Passover. Also living in the three-story house on Fitzwater Street were Anderson's aunt and cousins Queenie and Grace, as well as a few boarders. Soon enough, the entire extended family moved to larger quarters on Christian Street.

After graduating from grammar school, Anderson attended William Penn High School and, for practicality's sake, focused on commercial studies. The school offered her a music class once a week. Instead of taking voice lessons, she learned how to type and take dictation in the hopes of

■ *Strong-willed Isabella Anderson,*
Marian's grandmother.

ANNENBERG RARE BOOK AND
MANUSCRIPT LIBRARY, UNIVERSITY OF
PENNSYLVANIA

getting a job and helping her mother with household expenses. Her talent, though, could not be hidden; soon she was singing solos in the school chorus. Anderson's dream was starting to take shape. "I liked the key of E-flat for bright songs," she wrote in her memoir about this time in her life, "and I was attracted to the key of D-flat because it was so flattering to a low voice like mine. D-flat made me think of velvet."

In her teens, Anderson began to sing in the adult choir at church as well as the junior choir. The Union Baptist Church, her family's spiritual home, took an ever-increasing role in her singing. The congregation's support never faltered. Wanting to "do something for Marian," Reverend Wesley Parks took up a collection that raised $17.02. Anderson decided that she needed concert clothes and, rather than pay what they considered to be exorbitant prices at Wanamaker's department store, she and her mother bought satin fabric and made the dress themselves. "This was my dress for quite some time," Anderson would remember.

CAN'T I BE A SINGER BECAUSE I'M COLORED?

Anderson began to sing more and started to charge five dollars per appearance. Out of each five-dollar fee, she gave her mother two dollars, each of her sisters one dollar, and kept the remaining dollar for herself. She traveled by trolley to other churches to sing and made her first appearance with the Philadelphia Choral Society. She met Roland Hayes, a famous African-American tenor, whom she would later call her "hero." He began to take an interest in her career and suggested that she travel to Boston to study with his teacher, Arthur Hubbard. But Grandmother Anderson would have no part of this idea, so she stayed put. Hayes, however, came up with an acceptable alternative for Anderson, and she began to sing at black colleges and churches near Philadelphia.

In her late teens, still anxious to study at a real music school, Anderson found one in Philadelphia and went to enroll. She waited in line with the other applicants, but the young woman handing out applications ignored her until Anderson was the only one left. At that point, the woman asked her what she wanted, and Anderson answered that she wanted an application. "We don't take colored" was her reply.

■ *Marian Anderson, soloist for the Clef Club, at the Philadelphia Academy of Music, April 1918.* ANNENBERG RARE BOOK AND MANUSCRIPT LIBRARY, UNIVERSITY OF PENNSYLVANIA

■ *A segregated bus station in Memphis with separate areas for blacks and whites. Despite the Jim Crow laws, Anderson toured the South, where she was often greeted by prejudice. Still, Anderson swallowed the insults bitterly, hoping to teach by example. "I always bear in mind that my mission is to leave behind me the kind of impression that will make it easier for those who follow," she wrote.* LC-USZ62-129924

"I promise you," Anderson would later write about the incident, "I was as sick as if she'd hit me with her fist right in the middle of my stomach. . . . I wonder I didn't throw up right there. . . . All I could think of was how anybody who was as pretty as that, and had a chance to listen to music all day long, could act that way and say such a terrible thing. And then I'd think, 'Can't I sing, can't I be a singer because I'm colored?'"

It was a harsh lesson for Anderson—and, unfortunately, the first of many. When she would later travel to the South by train, she had to sit in the car marked "blacks only." The Jim Crow car was inevitably dirty, smoky, and sooty from being directly behind the train's engine. "I had heard about Jim Crow," Anderson recalled, "but meeting it bit deeply into the soul. . . . I had looked closely at my people in the train. Some seemed to be embarrassed to the core. Others appeared to accept the situation as if it were beyond repair."

Anderson, however, was undeterred. She wanted to venture forth into the world to share her gift, but not everybody was ready to accept an African-American singer, no matter how talented.

■ *Anderson, striking a dramatic pose in an evening gown, at the age of twenty-three.*
ANNENBERG RARE BOOK AND
MANUSCRIPT LIBRARY,
UNIVERSITY OF PENNSYLVANIA

"MY VOICE IS BEGINNING TO SPEAK IN A NEW WAY"

ANDERSON FOUND a teacher in her own neighborhood, the soprano Mary Saunders Patterson, and began to take voice lessons with her. Aware of the family's limited finances, Patterson taught the aspiring singer free of charge. Under her tutelage, Anderson learned how to control her voice, produce a certain tone, and project from the stage. Patterson also presented Anderson with her first "real evening gown" and introduced her to musician and accompanist Billy King, who would become Anderson's partner on her local tours. With Patterson's guidance, Anderson developed a taste and an eventual love for the songs of Franz Schubert.

■ *Anderson's friend and first accompanist, William "Billy" King, 1918. King was devoted to Anderson and played for her on her early tours of black churches and colleges.*
ANNENBERG RARE BOOK AND MANUSCRIPT LIBRARY, UNIVERSITY OF PENNSYLVANIA

■ *The community saw special potential in the young Anderson and rallied around her. G. Grant Williams, editor of the* Philadelphia Tribune*, ran an ad to promote a benefit concert "to assist in the musical education of Miss Marian E. Anderson." The concert took place on June 23, 1915, at the Musical Fund Hall in Philadelphia.*
ANNENBERG RARE BOOK AND MANUSCRIPT LIBRARY, UNIVERSITY OF PENNSYLVANIA

When Patterson realized that her pupil was ready for more advanced training, she recommended Agnes Reifsnyder, a local voice teacher who, like Anderson, was a contralto. The church and the black community helped raise the money for lessons. In June 1915, the People's Chorus held a benefit concert and raised funds to further Anderson's musical education.

Agnes Reifsnyder helped Anderson learn the proper breathing technique to make her singing stronger but more effortless. The two worked together until, once again, it was time to find another teacher. Dr. Lucy Langdon Wilson, the principal of South Philadelphia High School for Girls, to which Anderson had transferred, took a keen interest in her and arranged an audition with a voice teacher of some renown. At first, Giuseppe Boghetti, a colorful personality who had studios in Philadelphia and New York, wanted nothing to do with Anderson—until she sang the spiritual "Deep River" for him. He was so moved that he told her,

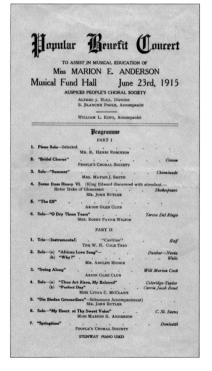

■ *The program for the June 1915 benefit concert included a solo performance by Anderson of a song from Camille Saint-Saëns'* Samson et Dalila. *Accompanist Billy King appeared on the program as well. "Music is such an elusive thing,"* Anderson once wrote. *"I may work on a song every day for a week while nothing much happens. Then suddenly there is a flash of understanding."*
ANNENBERG RARE BOOK AND MANUSCRIPT LIBRARY, UNIVERSITY OF PENNSYLVANIA

19

"I will make room for you right away." Boghetti promised Anderson that they would need to work together for only two years; after that, she would be able to sing anything—and everywhere—she chose. As it happened, teacher and student would stay together for much longer than that. The congregants at Union Baptist Church again stepped up to the plate, organizing a gala concert and raising about six hundred dollars for Anderson's lessons with Boghetti.

About the time she graduated from high school—June 20, 1921— Anderson began touring black churches and colleges, such as the Hampton Institute in Virginia and Howard University in Washington, DC, with Billy

■ *Anderson's graduating class, South Philadelphia High School for Girls, 1921. Anderson is in the second row from the top, second girl on the left.*

ANNENBERG RARE BOOK AND MANUSCRIPT LIBRARY, UNIVERSITY OF PENNSYLVANIA

■ *Jim Crow laws kept blacks segregated from whites on buses, on railroads, and in movie theaters. Here, an African-American man takes the stairs to the external entrance for "colored admission."* FSA 8A41115

King as her accompanist and sometime manager. Before long, she and King were able to command one hundred dollars per appearance, even if it did mean having to put up with segregated hotels, trains, drinking fountains, and theaters, which had special entrances for black patrons. Despite such humiliation, these appearances served to give Anderson a sense of self. "The more I sang, the more confident I became," she said about this time in her life. "My voice was beginning to speak in a new way."

With momentum building, Anderson thought it was time to take a leap artistically and arranged a concert at New York's famed Town Hall, a venue for distinguished concert artists. Though she was promised a full house, when the curtain opened on April 23, 1924, the seats were barely one-third filled. Her heart sank. The concert was not only poorly attended, it was poorly reviewed as well. One critic urged her to spend more time at her studies and less time on the concert stage. Her voice was praised, but her technique left the critics wondering if she had attempted too much too soon. Anderson took the criticism hard. "I felt lost and defeated. The dream was over," she said.

The feeling of defeat lasted months. Anderson had let nothing stand in her way—not her family's financial circumstances, nor the humiliating and degrading Jim Crow laws. The critics' stinging words, however, were another matter. She took occasional lessons with Boghetti, but he did not push her to work harder. She took comfort in her immediate family now that she, her mother, and her sisters were living in a little house they had bought with money that her mother had inherited, along with savings from Anderson's concerts: she gave approximately six hundred dollars toward the purchase of the home.

At this time, Anderson was being courted by a young man named Orpheus "King" Fisher, from a prominent Delaware family for whom she had sung. Fisher was persistent in his attentions: "Don't you think it's time we sent our clothes to the laundry in the same basket?" he asked provocatively. Apparently, Anderson liked her own basket well enough at this point, and put all her efforts into her career, which had just experienced its first major artistic bump.

But a bump was all it was—nothing that would interfere with the talent, momentum, and daring Anderson possessed. She entered a singing contest through the Philadelphia Philharmonic Society and took first prize, becoming the first African-American to do so and the first to appear with the Academy of Music.

"DOES 44A HAVE ANOTHER SONG?"

Boghetti entered Anderson and another student, soprano Reba Patton, in the Lewisohn Stadium concert competition, for the chance to appear as a soloist with the New York Philharmonic. On a summer day in 1925, the two young women took the train from Philadelphia to New York City and went to Boghetti's Park Avenue studio to practice, before heading to Aeolian Hall on Fifth Avenue. Patton was given the number 44, and Anderson, 44A. The judges sat in the balcony. They called each singer by number and sounded a loud clicker when they had heard enough. Most of the singers got "clicked" long before they finished their song, but Boghetti advised Anderson to keep singing until she finished her aria, no matter what. Though appreciative of the advice, she felt strongly that she would follow the rules and stop if she heard the clicker. By the time she was called to sing, six other contestants had sung the chosen aria: "O mio Fernando" from Donizetti's opera *La Favorita*. Anderson took the stage and sang the aria, including the final trill, with no sign of the clicker. In fact, she was greeted with applause by the other hopefuls, as she was the first allowed to complete her song. When the applause ended, a voice from the balcony asked, "Does 44A have another song?"

A few days later, back home in Philadelphia, Anderson learned that she was one of sixteen out of three hundred singers to make it as a semifinalist, and she returned to a hot and muggy New York City. Once again she sang "O mio Fernando," followed by two other songs. When she finished, she and Boghetti returned to his studio. Shortly after, the phone rang, and they learned the news that Anderson had won hands down; there would be no finals.

On August 26, 1925, Anderson took the stage with the New York Philharmonic at Lewisohn Stadium and won over her New York audience—a startling turnaround from her less-than-stellar Town Hall appearance. Now, she was a success; even the *New York Times* thought so:

> Miss Anderson made an excellent impression. She is endowed by nature with a voice of unusual compass, color, and dramatic capacity. The lower tones have a warm contralto quality, but the voice has the range and the resources of the mezzo-soprano. In passages of sustained melody the singer showed a feeling for melodic lines, while in the aria "O mio Fernando" she gave evidence of instructive dramatic impulse. Miss Anderson also sang Negro spirituals.

Her success also brought her to the attention of impresario Arthur Judson, who agreed to represent her.

26

MARIAN FEVER

ANDERSON WAS DRAWN to *Lieder*, the art songs of German composers and poets. "Morgen," by Richard Strauss, was one of her favorites, but she did not feel her German language skills were good enough to master it. Without *Lieder* in her repertoire, she would never be taken seriously as a concert singer. She began to hear other singers perform works by Robert Schumann, such as the song cycle *Frauenliebe und Leben,* and knew she must tackle them. At a private recital, she sang a song in German, but forgot some of the words and had to improvise. She felt her limitations keenly: "It kept haunting me and making me feel that I must find some way to become absolutely sure of my German." Europe had been calling Anderson for a while, only now it was a voice she could no longer ignore. As she told her mother, "I was going stale; I had to get away from my old haunts for a while; progress was at a standstill; repeating the same engagements each year, even if programs varied a little, was becoming routine; my career needed a fresh impetus, and perhaps a European stamp would help."

■ *A score of Bach's "Komm, süsser Tod" with notes in Anderson's hand. "Everyone has his favorites," Anderson said. "I suppose mine are 'Ave Maria,' 'Begrüssing,' 'Komm, süsser Tod,' Bach's 'Es ist vollbracht,' 'The Crucifixion,' and perhaps the most precious of all, 'He Has the Whole World in His Hands.'"*
ANNENBERG RARE BOOK AND MANUSCRIPT LIBRARY,
UNIVERSITY OF PENNSYLVANIA

With fifteen hundred dollars in traveler's checks and credit, as well as letters of introduction in her pocket, Anderson boarded the ocean liner *Ile de France* and set sail for England. It was 1927, only a few years before Hitler's policies would make her no longer welcome in Germany.

Many African-American artists of this period—including entertainer Josephine Baker and blues singer Alberta Hunter—had left the segregated United States and moved overseas in order to find acceptance. Anderson stayed at the London home of one such expatriate, John Payne, a singer and actor who had once visited her in Philadelphia. She studied *Lieder* with Raimund von Zur Mühlen and gave several performances that were well received. After a brief return home, she toured Europe in earnest with a grant from the Julius Rosenwald Fund.

"LONG LIVE MARIAN!"

This time, Anderson settled in Berlin with a German couple who, fortunately for her, spoke no English, so she had to learn German. She also began to study with voice teacher Kurt Johnen. After a time, she put up her own money—five hundred dollars' worth of American Express checks—to sing at the Bachsaal, a concert hall named for Johann Sebastian Bach in Leipzig. Her program included songs by Beethoven and Schubert, as well as her signature spirituals.

■ *Anderson leans over the piano to look at sheet music with her vocal coach Kurt Johnen, Berlin, 1931.* LC-USZ62-66162

Her investment paid off: the concert hall was full, the audience adoring, and the critics filled with praise. Even the concert manager was astonished by Anderson's talent, exclaiming, "I did not know I had such an artist. You are marvelous."

Marian Anderson may have won warm praise in Germany, but it was not until she sang in Scandinavia that she really caught fire. In addition to her beauty, breathtaking voice, and dramatic presence, her skin color was a bit of a rarity in Scandinavia. In fact, one reviewer described her as being "dressed in electric-blue satin and looking very much like a chocolate bar." Anderson acknowledged that this reaction had nothing to do with prejudice, but was based on pure wonderment. Her addition of native Scandinavian songs to her concert programs must have added to the puzzling picture.

Her accompanist at this time was Kosti Vehanen, a Finnish pianist and talent scout who had gone to see Anderson in Germany and had, in fact, encouraged this northern tour. Anderson credited Vehanen with "guiding me onto the path that led to my becoming an accepted international singer." Enthusiasm for Anderson was enormous. Crowds went wild for her; admirers flocked to the theater and sent flowers; critics raved about her performances; newspapers could not get enough of her. Everyone wanted to know more about this stunning American singer with the rich, deep voice. So huge was her popularity at this point that a newspaper coined the term "Marian Fever" for the spell Anderson cast. According to one paper, an Anderson concert in Denmark had ended with "people jump[ing] up on their chairs cheering and crying, 'Long live Marian!'"

Marian Anderson in Vienna, 1934.

LC-USZ62-66161

■ *Anderson stands at the bend of the concert grand after receiving flowers for a 1935 performance in Austria. Kosti Vehanen is her devoted accompanist.* ANNENBERG RARE BOOK AND MANUSCRIPT LIBRARY, UNIVERSITY OF PENNSYLVANIA

■ *Anderson's growing stature as a singer did not prevent her from raking hay with friend Thérèse Enwall in Finland, 1934. Enwall's husband, Helmer, was Anderson's European concert manager.* ANNENBERG RARE BOOK AND MANUSCRIPT LIBRARY, UNIVERSITY OF PENNSYLVANIA

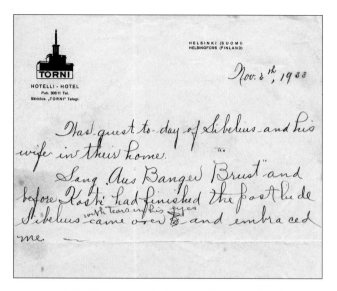

HELSINKI (SUOMI)
HELSINGFORS (FINLAND)

Nov. 6th, 1933

Was guest to-day of Sibelius and his wife in their home.

Sang "Aus Banger Brust" and before Kosti had finished the postlude Sibelius with tears in his eyes *came over and embraced me.*

■ *When "Marian Fever" was at its hottest, Anderson met famed composer Jean Sibelius at his home in Finland. Her note, scribbled on hotel stationery, records the event and Sibelius' emotional reaction to her performance of one of his own compositions, "Aus banger Brust."*
ANNENBERG RARE BOOK AND MANUSCRIPT LIBRARY, UNIVERSITY OF PENNSYLVANIA

Vehanen arranged for Anderson to meet Finnish composer Jean Sibelius at his home, Villa Ainola, near Helsinki. After she sang some of his songs, he told her, "My roof is too low for your voice." He embraced Anderson, and with that the scheduled refreshment of coffee was turned into a cry for champagne. Sibelius would later dedicate his song "Solitude" to her.

■ *Russian avant-garde theater director Konstantin Stanislavsky (left) seems awestruck at Anderson's performance in Russia, January 1935. Stanislavsky wanted Anderson to sing the title role in his production of the opera* Carmen, *but she declined to stay in Moscow due to the demands of her touring schedule. Anderson later regretted her decision, saying, "It would have been wise to grasp that opportunity even at the expense of postponing the tour."* ANNENBERG RARE BOOK AND MANUSCRIPT LIBRARY, UNIVERSITY OF PENNSYLVANIA

After Scandinavia, Anderson performed in many of the major capitals of Europe, including Paris, where she caught the attention of Sol Hurok, the most famous impresario of the time. He was a larger-than-life figure whom Anderson described as being "built along generous proportions." When she and Vehanen arrived at Hurok's office the day after he had attended one of her recitals, the impresario was sitting in a big chair with his cane on a desk in front of him. Soon, Hurok uttered the magic words: "I might be able to do something for you." After clearing her obligations with the Judson Agency, she signed on with Hurok, beginning a fruitful relationship that would last until his death in the 1960s.

Hurok's was not the only internationally renowned voice to praise Anderson. In Austria, her performances during the 1935 Salzburg Festival drew the attention of maestro Arturo Toscanini, who told Anderson that "yours is a voice such as one hears once in a hundred years." Anderson was so thrilled to meet Toscanini that she had to rely on others who were present that evening to recount the event. "The sight of him caused my heart to leap and throb so violently that I did not hear a word he said." The world, however, was listening; Marian Anderson had officially arrived.

In 1935, she returned to the States and began touring under the management of Hurok. But there was great concern about who would be her accompanist. Kosti Vehanen had just toured with her in Europe and knew most of her recent work. He had seen her mature as an artist. Billy King, however, was an old friend who had accompanied her at her earliest concerts. If she made a choice based on artistic merit, she would choose

■ *Anderson became the toast of Europe during the years she lived and performed there. Here, she stands alone on the stage of the Paris Opera on December 14, 1937, captivating her audience with her song.* ANNENBERG RARE BOOK AND MANUSCRIPT LIBRARY, UNIVERSITY OF PENNSYLVANIA

Vehanen. If old family ties and friendship were the deciding factor, then she would choose King. And if race figured into her decision—and it most certainly did—she would have to anticipate the reaction of a southern audience raised on Jim Crow to a white man playing for a black woman. Anderson dared to choose the best candidate, and Vehanen was delighted to have the job.

Their first challenge—professional and psychological—was a December 30 engagement at Town Hall in New York, the scene of one of Anderson's few failures. They began preparing for the concert while still in

THE TOWN HALL

123 WEST 43rd STREET, NEW YORK, N. Y.

MARIAN ANDERSON

Alfred Scott • Publisher • 156 Fifth Avenue, New York

100-12-30E-35

Europe and throughout the journey home across the Atlantic. Aboard ship one day, Anderson lost her balance when the boat tossed. She slipped and broke her ankle. At the New York appearance, no one in the audience knew that underneath her elegant gown, Anderson's foot was in a cast. Typically, singer and accompanist make an entrance together, so it must have seemed odd that Anderson and Vehanen were already on stage when the curtain parted. Unlike her previous performance at Town Hall, this one—from her first notes of Handel's "Begrüssing"—was a hit, as music critic Harold Taubman reported in the *New York Times*:

> Let it be said at the outset: Marian Anderson has returned to her native land one of the great singers of our time. The Negro contralto who has been abroad for four years established herself in her concert at the Town Hall last night as the possessor of an excelling voice and art. Her singing enchanted an audience that included singers. There was no doubt of it, she was mistress of all she surveyed.

■ *The program for Marian Anderson's triumphant return to Town Hall in New York, December 30, 1935. Anderson sang works by Handel, Schubert, Verdi, and Sibelius, as well as spirituals.*

MAKING AND SINGING HISTORY

OF ALL ANDERSON'S appearances, one has achieved iconic status, not just for *how* it happened but *why.* It shook a nation; it soothed a nation; and, ultimately, it changed a nation. Though she was a classical concert artist first, her 1939 performance at the Lincoln Memorial made her a symbol for the burgeoning civil rights movement. Anderson, who was not overtly political, stepped easily into the role. "You can not accomplish anything if you run away from it," she once said. "But I think if you have something to offer to help a situation . . . then I think you should do it in your own manner."

It all started when Sol Hurok wanted to bring Anderson to Washington, DC, and chose Constitution Hall, owned by the patriotic Daughters of the American Revolution (DAR), as the largest and most appropriate venue for her. Anderson had played the capital before, appearing at Howard University, but now she was more popular than ever. The DAR, however, denied their hall to Anderson because she was black and their policy forbade them from renting it to African-Americans. Hurok had no luck convincing them to reverse their decision; the DAR would not budge. As in Nazi Germany, where Anderson had been denied a concert in Berlin for not being Aryan, here in her own beloved America, she was turned away by a concert hall because of the color of her skin. Howard University, a historically black institution, decided to challenge the DAR's "whites only" policy, as well as Jim Crow laws in Washington, DC.

■ *Anderson receives an honorary doctorate of music from Howard University in Washington, DC, 1938.* ANNENBERG RARE BOOK AND MANUSCRIPT LIBRARY, UNIVERSITY OF PENNSYLVANIA

At the time of these deeply sensitive negotiations, Anderson was in San Francisco, far away from the fray. There, she was surprised to see the following newspaper headline: "Mrs. Roosevelt Takes Stand: Resigns from DAR." A media frenzy ensued. In the lobby of her hotel, Anderson spoke briefly to reporters and said, "I am shocked beyond words to be barred from the capital of my own country after having appeared in almost every other capital in the world."

Eleanor Roosevelt must have felt the singer's humiliation. Anderson had previously sung for the Roosevelts at the White House, and the two women would strike up a lifelong friendship based on respect and mutual understanding. Roosevelt had even written about Anderson's White House performance in her syndicated *My Day* newspaper column:

> My husband and I had a rare treat Wednesday night in listening to Marian Anderson, a colored contralto, who has made a great success in Europe and this country. She has sung before nearly all the crowned heads, and deserves her great success, for I have rarely heard a more beautiful and moving voice or a more finished artist.

Walter White, executive secretary of the National Association for the Advancement of Colored People (NAACP) and a close friend of Eleanor Roosevelt, contributed to the effort to bring Anderson to Washington, sending letters to members of the musical, artistic, and cultural communities asking for support. With the doors to Constitution Hall barred to Anderson, the offer of a free outdoor concert at the Lincoln Memorial was formally made by Harold Ickes, secretary of the interior. When the idea was mentioned to President Roosevelt, he replied, "I don't care if she sings from the top of the Washington Monument, as long as she sings."

Early on the morning of April 9, 1939—Easter Sunday—Anderson and her mother arrived from Philadelphia and went straight to the home of Gifford Pinchot, former governor of Pennsylvania. Ironically, no hotel

■ *At the famed Lincoln Memorial concert, Marian Anderson's first words from the song "America" were "My country 'tis of thee, sweet land of liberty, of thee we sing."*
LC-USZ62-90448

would take them, despite Anderson's status as a leading singer. A few hours before the concert, she and Kosti Vehanen went to the Lincoln Memorial to try out the piano and the public address system. When all was found to be in working order, they left and returned later in the afternoon. This would be one of the last times Anderson and Vehanen would play together, for he returned to Finland in 1940.

Howard University and Associated Sponsors

PRESENT

MARIAN ANDERSON

AT

THE LINCOLN MEMORIAL

IN

WASHINGTON

Sunday, April 9, 1939

FIVE O'CLOCK

*"Fourscore and seven years ago our fathers brought forth on
this continent a new nation, conceived in liberty and dedicated
to the proposition that all men are created equal."*

ABRAHAM LINCOLN.

On the platform were dignitaries, senators, and members of Congress, as well as a Supreme Court justice. The audience of seventy-five thousand extended well beyond the Washington Monument. Boy Scouts, both black and white, distributed the printed program with lines from Lincoln's Gettysburg Address. "I had a feeling that a great wave of good will poured out from these people, almost engulfing me," Anderson recalled. "And when I stood up to sing our national anthem I felt for a moment as though I were choking. For a desperate second I thought that the words, well as I know them, would not come."

But they came. When she sang "America," she changed the words "Of thee I sing" to "Of thee we sing." By the time she concluded with three spirituals, she had moved not only the audience in front of her but also those listening at home. For an encore, she sang another spiritual,

■ An Incident in
Contemporary American
Life, *a 1942 mural by Mitchell
Jamieson commemorating
Anderson's concert at the Lincoln
Memorial, still hangs at the
Department of the Interior
building in Washington, DC.*
COURTESY US DEPARTMENT OF
THE INTERIOR MUSEUM,
WASHINGTON, DC.
PHOTOGRAPH BY DAVID ALLISON

"Nobody Knows the Trouble I See."
When she had sung her last note and
gazed at the mass audience one last
time, she said, "I am so overwhelmed. I
just can't talk. I can't tell you what you
have done for me today. I thank you
from the bottom of my heart again and again."

Harold Ickes would later write, "I have never heard such a voice." And
with the voice came a message. The concert was immensely symbolic, as
she sang in front of the statue of Abraham Lincoln, insisting on the truth
of his words in the Gettysburg Address, that "all men are created equal."
Anderson, who normally shunned controversy and politics, had let herself
become an instrument of change, accepting the job with grace, passion,
and conviction. ■

THE VOICE HEARD 'ROUND THE WORLD

ANDERSON CONTINUED to seek out new challenges and was rewarded with new accolades. In 1939, she was awarded the Spingarn Medal from the NAACP. Established in 1914, the Spingarn acknowledges outstanding achievements by African-Americans. Later recipients have included Rosa Parks, Maya Angelou, and Colin Powell. In 1941, Anderson received the ten-thousand-dollar Philadelphia Award, established twenty years earlier by editor and author Edward W. Bok, for her contributions to the city. She used the money to establish the Marian Anderson Scholarship Fund to help emerging singers blessed with talent but not necessarily sufficient means. More than sixty years later, the scholarship fund is still going strong.

During World War II, Anderson sang for the troops. The DAR, who had denied her the opportunity to sing in Constitution Hall, now asked her to perform at a benefit concert. She agreed, but only if the audience would not be segregated. The January 7, 1943, concert was the first held at Constitution Hall without any kind of segregated seating.

That same year, Anderson married her longtime sweetheart, Orpheus Fisher. The couple bought a one-hundred-acre farm in Danbury, Connecticut, which they named Marianna Farm. Fisher, an architect, began to make improvements to the property, including the construction of a rehearsal studio where Anderson could prepare for upcoming appearances. Here, she could also relax with her family and indulge in favorite

■ *Marian Anderson receives the Spingarn Medal from Eleanor Roosevelt, July 2, 1939. "She is one of the most admirable human beings I have ever met. . . . I suspect that she has done a great deal for people that [has] never been divulged publicly. I know what she did for me," Anderson said of Eleanor Roosevelt, with whom she formed a lifelong friendship.*
LC-USZ62-116730

pastimes such as cooking, sewing, and photography. Outside her home, Anderson continued to encounter racial discrimination, as when one theater manager insisted that she not hold the hand of her white accompanist, Franz Rupp, when they walked across the stage. The audience, however, felt differently, as Anderson observed: "We went off and returned, and this time, as is my custom, I took my accompanist's hand. For a split second the house was quiet, and then there was a deafening outburst of applause."

■ *Marian Anderson traveled around the world to sing for appreciative audiences. Here, she is about to board a jet in the 1940s.* ANNENBERG RARE BOOK AND MANUSCRIPT LIBRARY, UNIVERSITY OF PENNSYLVANIA

In the 1950s, Anderson decided that she would no longer sing before segregated audiences. Times were changing. Amidst the prejudice and hate that gripped the South, Dr. Martin Luther King Jr. was preaching his message of nonviolence. It was time for Anderson to take a firm stand:

> I was never happy about singing in halls where segregation was practiced. Several years ago I decided that I had had enough, and I made it a rule that I would not sing where there was segregation. I am aware that this decision made it difficult for the sponsors of local concerts in some cities where I had appeared. They did not feel that they could venture to present concerts on any basis other than the old one—with an invisible line marking off the Negro section from orchestra to topmost balcony.

ONE WHO SAID YES

In 1955, Anderson was presented with a new opportunity and challenge: she was invited to appear with the Metropolitan Opera in New York by general manager Rudolf Bing. By accepting, she became the first African-American singer ever to appear on the Met's stage. Once again, Anderson was chosen to break new ground. Though her stage time was brief, the Met engagement opened the doors to African-American singers, who had been barred from many of the best venues. That same year, 1955, also saw Rosa Parks' refusal

■ *Marian Anderson and Orpheus "King" Fisher finally tie the knot, July 1943, at Marianna Farm, their estate near Danbury, Connecticut.*

ANNENBERG RARE BOOK AND MANUSCRIPT LIBRARY, UNIVERSITY OF PENNSYLVANIA

■ *Anderson rehearses with a professional sound and camera crew at Marianna Farm. Singers, family, and friends would also gather at Marian and Orpheus' home.*
ANNENBERG RARE BOOK AND MANUSCRIPT LIBRARY, UNIVERSITY OF PENNSYLVANIA

■ *Anderson rehearses with conductor Leonard Bernstein at Lewisohn Stadium, New York, 1947.* COURTESY RUTH ORKIN ARCHIVE. LIBRARY OF CONGRESS MUSIC DIVISION, LBPHOTOS 47A119

to give up her seat on a segregated bus, leading to the Montgomery bus boycott. The two women, Anderson and Parks—one who said yes, and one who said no—helped define the times.

Bing chose for Anderson the role of the sorceress Ulrica in Verdi's opera *Un Ballo in Maschera* (The Masked Ball). Conducted by Dimitri Mitropoulos, the opera also starred soprano Zinka Milanov and tenor

■ *One of the leading actors of his day, Paul Robeson was an outspoken activist who demanded civil rights for all people—in contrast to Anderson, who preferred to soldier on silently and teach by example. Here, Robeson performs one of his signature roles, Othello.*

Richard Tucker. Anderson's appearance was life changing, as she recalled in her memoir: "The chance to be a member of the Metropolitan has been a highlight of my life. It has meant much to me and to my people." Her only regret about this experience is that it did not come earlier in her life. She was nearing sixty when she stepped into the role of Ulrica, with very little stage acting under her belt.

■ *Legendary conductor of the Philadelphia Orchestra Leopold Stokowski conducts the Westminster Choir College Choir as Marian Anderson sings "Ave Maria" for a filmed Christmas concert, 1944.*

ANNENBERG RARE BOOK AND MANUSCRIPT LIBRARY, UNIVERSITY OF PENNSYLVANIA

■ *Marian Anderson shares the stage with Rudolf Bing, celebrated manager of the Metropolitan Opera, 1954.* ANNENBERG RARE BOOK AND MANUSCRIPT LIBRARY, UNIVERSITY OF PENNSYLVANIA

Never one to rest on her accomplishments, Anderson toured India and the Far East in 1957 at the behest of the State Department. She also spent time in Israel, where she established a fund for young singers. Being in the Holy Land was especially important to Anderson, whose faith and love of spirituals seemed to bring her to this point. The following year, she was appointed as a delegate to the United Nations by President Eisenhower and assigned to the Trusteeship Council, which oversaw territories in central Africa and the southwestern Pacific.

■ *When Anderson returned home to Philadelphia in 1954 to dedicate the Marian Anderson Recreation Center at Seventeenth and Fitzwater streets,* Look *magazine did a special feature on her. For the article, Anderson was photographed where she got her start—singing in the Union Baptist Church.*

The turbulent 1960s brought Anderson back to Washington, DC, where she sang at President Kennedy's inaugural. Three years later, she attended the historic March on Washington for Jobs and Freedom, the occasion of Dr. King's famous "I have a dream" speech, which drew more than two hundred thousand people. Anderson found herself once again in front of the Lincoln Memorial, singing her signature spiritual "He's Got the Whole World in His Hands."

■ *Anderson rehearses her role as the sorceress Ulrica in Verdi's* Un Ballo in Maschera *on the stage of the famed Metropolitan Opera in New York City.*

■ *Marian Anderson as Ulrica in* Un Ballo in Maschera. *Her debut at the Metropolitan Opera on January 7, 1955, broke racial barriers and paved the way for singers such as Leontyne Price, Shirley Verrett, and Jessye Norman.*

■ Look *magazine published this photo of Anderson and accompanist Franz Rupp receiving a warm welcome in Japan in 1953.* LOOK MAGAZINE COLLECTION, LIBRARY OF CONGRESS. PHOTOGRAPH COURTESY UNIVERSITY OF PENNSYLVANIA

Awards were continually bestowed on Anderson. In 1963, shortly after the assassination of President Kennedy, Lyndon Johnson presented her with the Presidential Medal of Freedom. In 1978, she won a Congressional Gold Medal. But above all, Anderson made her mark as a singer. Her voice captivated and inspired young people around the nation. Soprano Jessye Norman recalls hearing Anderson's voice for the first time at age ten: "It was a revelation. And I wept." In the early 1960s, the sixteen-year-old Norman took the train from Augusta, Georgia, to Philadelphia to

■ *Anderson rehearses* A Lincoln Portrait *with Aaron Copland, 1976. This 1942 work by the American composer broke new ground by setting excerpts from the writings of Abraham Lincoln to symphonic music. In her role as narrator, Anderson recited Lincoln's stirring words "As I would not be a slave, so I would not be a master. This expresses my idea of democracy. Whatever differs from this, to the extent of the difference, is no democracy." Having sung at the Lincoln Memorial in 1939 and again at the March on Washington in 1963, she was symbolically tied to the sixteenth president.*

PHOTOGRAPH BY ALLEN T. WINIGRAD. COURTESY AARON COPLAND MUSIC FUND. LIBRARY OF CONGRESS MUSIC DIVISION, COPLAND PHOT0042

■ *The Marian Anderson stamp, issued in 2005 for Black Heritage Month.*

COURTESY U.S. POSTAL SERVICE.

participate in the Marian Anderson Voice Competition. Though she did not win, she remained in awe of Anderson for her entire life: "She wore the glorious crown of her voice with the grace of an empress and changed the lives of many through the subtle force of her spirit and demeanor. If the planet Earth could sing, I think it would sound something like Marian Anderson."

Anderson lived an extraordinary life, onstage as well as off. When it was time for her to retire, she gave the last performance of her farewell tour on Easter Sunday 1965 at Carnegie Hall. She was nearly seventy years old and would now spend more time at Marianna Farm.

Her husband, Orpheus, died in 1985, and on April 8, 1993, Marian Anderson died at the age of ninety-six. For a woman who dared to use her voice to create beauty and change the world, a silent piano and flowers marked the memorial service at Carnegie Hall. ■

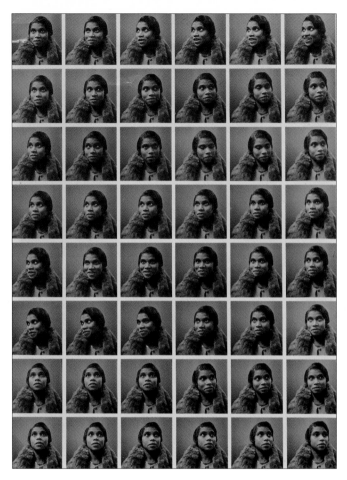

■ *The many faces of Marian Anderson—forty-eight images from a contact sheet, possibly taken in Geneva, Switzerland, c. 1934.*

ANNENBERG RARE BOOK AND MANUSCRIPT LIBRARY, UNIVERSITY OF PENNSYLVANIA

FURTHER READING AND SOURCES

Anderson, Marian. *My Lord, What a Morning*. New York: Viking Press, 1956. Reprinted with a new foreword by James DePreist. Urbana, IL: University of Illinois Press, 2002.

Freedman, Russell. *The Voice That Challenged a Nation: Marian Anderson and the Struggle for Equal Rights*. New York: Clarion Books, 2004.

Keiler, Allan. *Marian Anderson: A Singer's Journey*. New York: Scribner, 2000.

Ryan, Pam Muñoz. *When Marian Sang: The True Recital of Marian Anderson*. Illustrations by Brian Selznick. New York: Scholastic Press, 2002.

Vehanen, Kosti. *Marian Anderson: A Portrait*. New York: McGraw-Hill, 1941. Reprint, Westport, CT: Greenwood Press, 1970.

The most complete source of information on Anderson—in text, image, and sound—was compiled by the University of Pennsylvania's Annenberg Rare Book and Manuscript Library. The online exhibition, curated by Nancy M. Shawcross, can be accessed at www.library.upenn.edu/exhibits/rbm/anderson/.

Other informative websites include the Marian Anderson Historical Society (www.mariananderson.org); a remembrance of Anderson from the PBS program *NewsHour* (www.pbs.org/newshour/bb/remember/1997/anderson_2-26a.html); and an audiovisual biography presented by the Metropolitan Opera (www.marian-anderson.org/timeline.htm).

ACKNOWLEDGMENTS

The author would like to express his gratitude to Amy Pastan, series editor, for her ideas and enthusiasm and to Elaine Graalfs and Theresa Duran of Pomegranate for putting together such a beautiful publication. Thanks also to W. Ralph Eubanks and the Publications Office of the Library of Congress. Nancy Shawcross and John Pollack at the University of Pennsylvania provided many of the photographs from their fine collection.

This book is for Judith Jamison, inspirer, and Paul Szilard, my impresario.

IMAGES

Reproduction numbers, when available, are given for all items in the collections of the Library of Congress. Unless otherwise noted, Library of Congress images are from the Prints and Photographs Division. To order reproductions, note the LC- number provided with the image; where no number exists, note the Library division and the title of the item. Direct your request to:

The Library of Congress
Photoduplication Service
Washington DC 20540-4570
(202) 707-5640; www.loc.gov